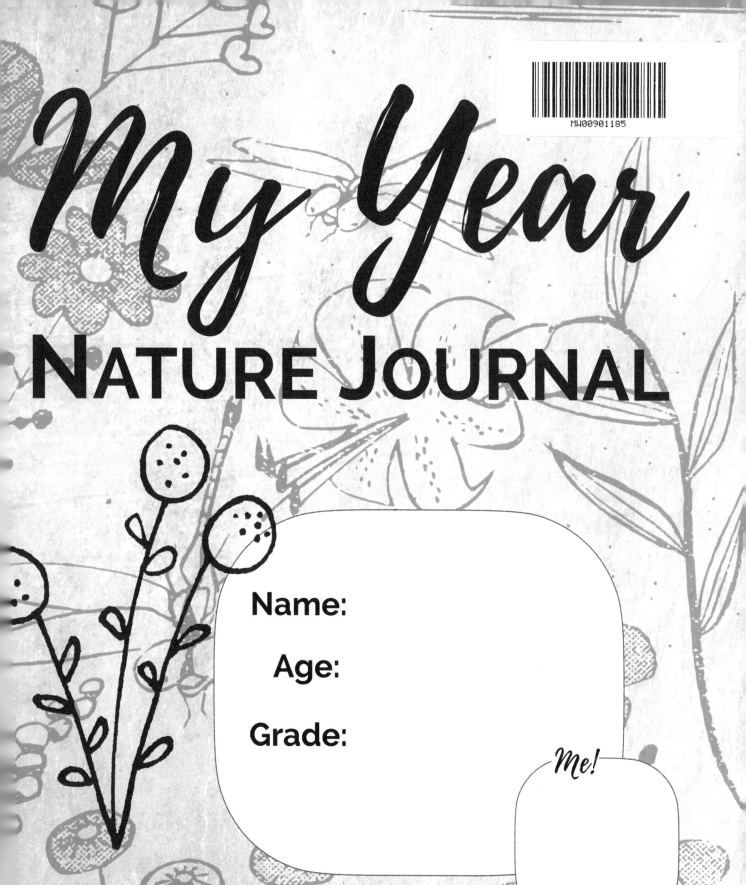

My Year
Nature Journal

Name:

Age:

Grade:

Me!

Rebecca Grabill

My Year
NATURE JOURNAL

Grabill Creative

First Printing, 2020

ISBN 9798556035799

Grabill Creative
Michigan, USA

www.rebeccagrabill.com

Contents

Inside My Year Nature Journal

Notes

Overview
About My Year Nature Journal

Topics Covered:

Seasons
Observation
Five Senses
Writing

Color Wheel
Spiders
Leaves & Trees
Clouds
Hibernation
Water Cycle
Nocturnal Animals
Animal Tracks
Seeds & Flowers
Weather
Habitats
& Much More!!!

The *My Year Nature Journal* guides you through a full year of nature study with lessons inspired by the picture book, *A Year With Mama Earth*.

Each month I've created a journal page to accompany a suggested Mini Adventure—time to experience and enjoy the natural world. If a page is likely to be messy (glue, paints, markers) I've placed a blank page behind it, so none of your creations will be ruined by page bleed-through. I've also included blank grid pages for notes and drawings of your own between each month.

- Supplies: Crayons, pencils, markers, watercolor paints, other craft supplies, glue, magnifying glass, tweezers, baggies. Optional: Magnifying bug box, clipboard, bag or backpack, water bottle.

- Focus on the *experience*. This journal is appropriate for PreK/Kindergarten (with assistance) to 4th grade or beyond, but the real treasure is the time spent exploring our intricate and amazing world!

- Paste a photo on the inside title page and add the year to the spine to make this journal a keepsake for years to come.

- Choose a day each week for your nature walk and bring your journal, small baggies (for treasures, which are sometimes messy!), and drawing supplies. Each month has enough journal pages to do one page each week, along with a Month page and Writer's Corner to be completed at home or in the classroom.

- Work to avoid disturbing habitats—part of enjoying nature is treating it with respect. Our home is also home to countless precious creatures!

Notes

January

Wintery Wonderland

This Month

Snow
Winter Animals
Birds
Shelter
Verbs

Silent deer grow brave in January,.

—From A Year With Mama Earth

What would you wear to hide in winter?

Winter

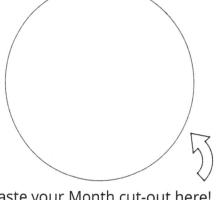

Paste your Month cut-out here!

January

Notes for Teachers

January topics:

Snow
Winter Animals
Birds
Shelter
Verbs

*Silent deer grow brave
in January,.*
—From A Year With Mama Earth

January, when everything begins anew. Resolutions, reflection, hopes and plans abound. Why not add a new goal of exploring outside at least once a week? I hope January's Journal pages can help you!

Find suggestions for each activity page below.

• January: Trace the word *Winter* and dress your monthly self-portrait to blend in with your local winter environment. Talk about camouflage and adaptation (this topic will be revisited in March).

• Birds Abound: Go on a winter scavenger hunt for birds common in your area.

• Make a Nest: Nests provide shelter for many types of animals. They often have several layers for different purposes—protection, camouflage, and finally, insulation.

• Snowgazing: You probably know that every snowflake is unique, but the diversity of flakes is truly amazing. Take a close look and practice magnifying-glass skills.

• Shelter: Shelter is important for all creatures, especially those who live in harsh climates. Match these animals to their shelters and label from the word bank.

• Make-It: Build a DIY wilderness shelter. Find videos and instructions on my website.

• Winter Food: The ultimate sustainable art! Find links to detailed instructions at rebeccagrabill.com.

• Writer's Corner: Verbs, verbs, verbs! Choose an action word, and draw/write about doing that action. Be as wild, wacky, creative as you like!

Birds Abound

A Scavenger Hunt

As you walk, check off the birds you see. Search by bird type, color, location, or draw/paste pictures of birds common in your area!

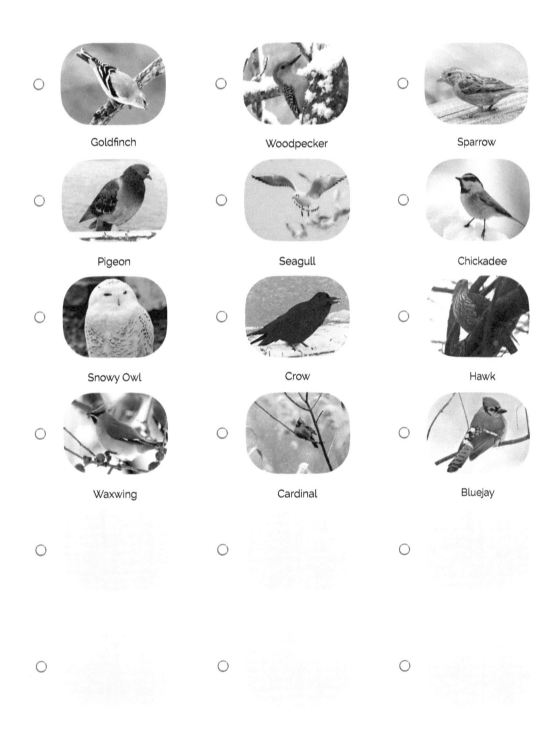

○ Goldfinch

○ Woodpecker

○ Sparrow

○ Pigeon

○ Seagull

○ Chickadee

○ Snowy Owl

○ Crow

○ Hawk

○ Waxwing

○ Cardinal

○ Bluejay

○

○

○

○

○

○

Make a Nest
Indoors or Out

What does a nest need to do? It should keep you warm, dry, and safe. How would you build a nest? Make one outside, or from blankets indoors. Draw your plan for the perfect nest below!

Shelter

Warm in the Wild

Match each winter creature with its shelter and label from the word bank below.

Drey—Squirrel

Home—People

Burrow—Rabbit

Den—Wolf

Forest—Deer

Nest—Bird (Cardinal)

Word Bank

Nest   Forest   Drey   Home   Den   Burrow

Make-It

DIY Shelter

Do you know how to build your own wilderness shelter? Working alone or as a group try to create one. Draw and describe it below.

My Shelter

Snowgazing
Up Close

Draw snow:

With a magnifying glass, I see:

How does your snowflake compare

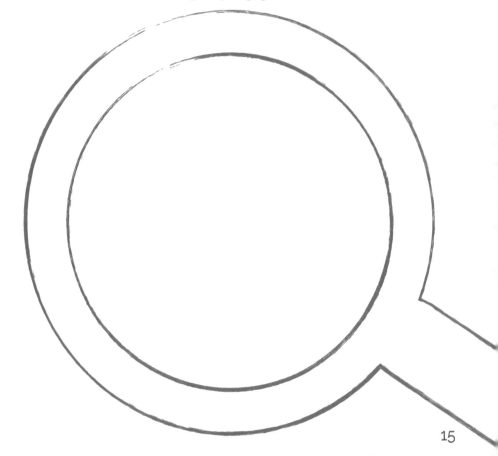

Winter Food

Ice Collage Feeder

How to make your own Hanging Ice Collage Bird Feeder:

1. Gather supplies—shallow pan (pie tin, cake pan, plastic frisbee, etc.), dried berries, birdseed, leaves, acorns, and other natural items. Durable cord for hanging.
2. Pour water in your pan.
3. Arrange seed and other natural items. Place cord looped with both ends in the water.
4. Allow to freeze.
5. Remove (you may have to place in warm water briefly).
6. Hang outdoors and watch birds enjoy!

Sketch your collage here:

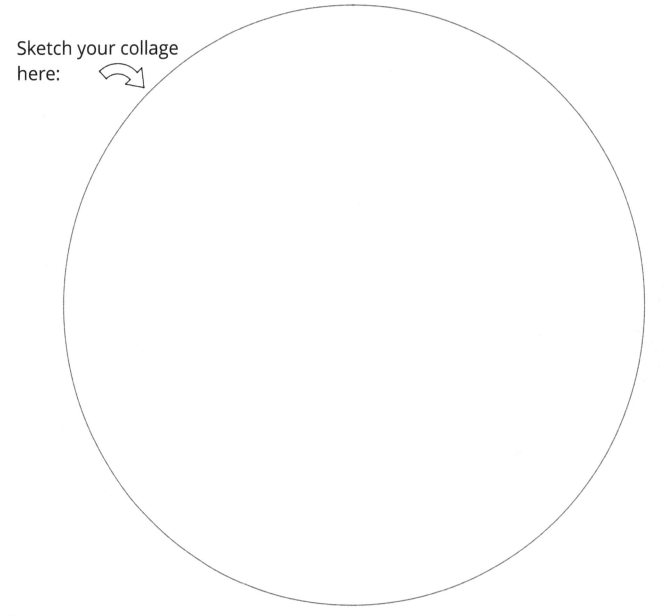

Writer's Corner
Draw & Write

If I could...

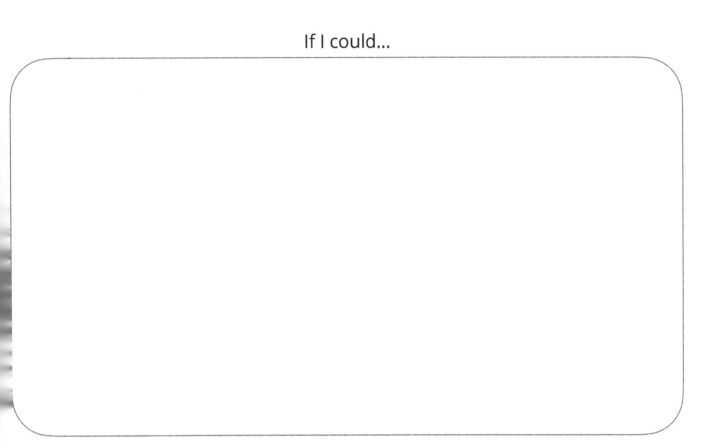

Choose an Action Word (Verb) and draw yourself doing it! Write about your day.

February

We Love Winter!

This Month

Night Animals
Animal Tracks
States of Matter
Characterization

By February, even the sparrows shiver, heads together, wings tucked tight.

—From *A Year With Mama Earth*

Look at My Shoes!

Valentine

Paste your Month cut-out here!

February

Notes for Teachers

February topics:

Night Animals
Animal Tracks
States of Matter
Characterization

By February, even the sparrows shiver, heads together, wings tucked tight.

—From *A Year With Mama Earth*

February, with hopes for spring, but very few signs of that mysterious sprite. Instead of surviving winter, let's dress in layers and explore! Some animal activity is easier to see in the cold months—fewer leaves to block views, tracks made clear by fresh snow (or mud or sand ... the deep midwinter wears different clothes in different parts of the world), so grab your pages and head outside!

Find suggestions for each activity page below.

- February: Trace the word *Valentine* and focus on your monthly self-portrait's shoes. What would your tracks look like?

- Snow Tracks: Whether you have snow, sand, or mud this time of year, you can hunt for animal tracks. Find one and add your sketch. What do your tracks look like?

- What is it?: Imagine you're out for a hike and see the weirdest tracks you've ever seen. What do they look like? What real or imagined animal do they belong to?

- Pop Quiz!: Did you know some animals we consider nocturnal actually aren't? That's right! Take this quiz (and check out rebeccagrabill.com) to find out more!

- States: Of matter, that is. If you're unfamiliar with states of matter, now is the time for an introduction. Then find examples of each state as you hike.

- Snow Maze: A favorite outdoor activity for any season is to create a life-sized maze out of snow (or sticks, leaves, etc.)

- Heart Hunt: February means Valentine's Day. Whether or not you celebrate, nature shares its love all year long—with hearts. Also discuss the art concept of negative space.

- Writer's Corner: What a character! Create your own creature! Describe, draw, and imagine.

Snow Tracks
Following Footprints

Can you find any of these tracks?

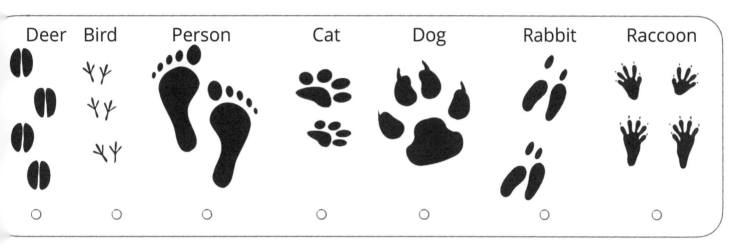

Deer	Bird	Person	Cat	Dog	Rabbit	Raccoon
○	○	○	○	○	○	○

I found tracks! They look like:

My animal might be:

These are MY tracks:

What is it!

Character Creation

You've seen animal tracks, now invent your own! Draw some tracks below.

The rest of my creature looks like this:

Four words to describe my creature:

- ○
- ○
- ○
- ○

My creature's habitat:

Pop Quiz!

Nocturnal — or Not

Do you know which animals below are **nocturnal** (active during the night), **diurnal** (active during the day), or **crepuscular** (active at dawn and twilight)? Quiz yourself to find out!

A

the rabbit is ...

1. nocturnal
2. diurnal
3. crepuscular

B

the raccoon is ...

1. nocturnal
2. diurnal
3. crepuscular

C

the skunk is ...

1. nocturnal
2. diurnal
3. crepuscular

D

the coyote is ...

1. nocturnal
2. diurnal
3. crepuscular

E

the deer is ...

1. nocturnal
2. diurnal
3. crepuscular

F

the chicken is...

1. nocturnal
2. diurnal
3. crepuscular

G

bats are ...

1. nocturnal
2. diurnal
3. crepuscular

H

people are ...

1. nocturnal
2. diurnal
3. crepuscular

I

cows are ...

1. nocturnal
2. diurnal
3. crepuscular

Answers: A3; B1; C3; D1; E3; F2; G1; H2; I2

What does Crepuscular mean?

The word *crepuscular* (cre-puss-cue-ler) comes from a Latin word meaning "twilight." Animals that are most active at dawn or dusk are not strictly diurnal or nocturnal. They are crepuscular!

29

States
Of Matter

Do you know the three states of matter? Liquid, solid, and gas. As you walk, look for something in each state.

Liquid

Solid

Gas

Snow Maze

A**maz**ing!

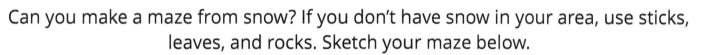

Can you make a maze from snow? If you don't have snow in your area, use sticks, leaves, and rocks. Sketch your maze below.

Heart Hunt

Hearts in Nature

If you look closely, the heart shape is everywhere in nature. Below are a few examples. What hearts can you find in nature?

Hearts in Nature

Negative Space

Negative space is the space around and between objects. Here the heart isn't created by the rock, but by the light and water.

How many hearts can you find? Use Tally marks to keep track.

Writer's Corner

Draw & Write

What a Character!

Draw and describe your character.

March
Where is Spring Hiding?

This Month

Textures
Camouflage vs. Mimicry
Trees & Soil
Story Structure

In March, Mama Earth leaves a layer of mud beneath the snow to dress the snowman on the lawn.
—From A Year With Mama Earth

I'm an animal (or plant)!

Textures

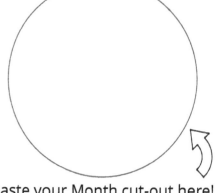

Paste your Month cut-out here!

March

Notes for Teachers

March topics:

Textures
Camouflage vs. Mimicry
Trees & Soil
Story Structure

In March, Mama Earth leaves a layer of mud beneath the snow to dress the snowman on the lawn.

—From A Year With Mama Earth

March roars in like a lion, and in many places, leaves like one, too. But often, spring tiptoes in on doe's hooves, breathing just enough warmth to wake the sleepy crocus. I hope you'll seek *and find* some whispers of spring as you explore outside this month.

Find suggestions for each activity page below.

- March: Talk about textures and draw yourself dressed in an animal or plant texture of your choice.

- Bark Walk: Make rubbings of different tree trunks and observe how the textures are different.

- Camouflage: Camouflage involves blending with surroundings while mimicry occurs when an animal looks like another part of nature to hide. Can you find examples of each?

- Adopt-a-Tree: Look forward to Arbor day (actually in April) by planting a tree or studying a favorite tree. New vocabulary might include *Crown, Bole,* and *Dormant.*

- Soil! Did you know that soil contains hundreds of living organisms? Collect a sample of soil and examine it with a magnifying glass. If available, look for signs of life with a microscope. The experiment suggested demonstrates just how many different textures and substances are in one spoon of soil.

- Worm Story: Discuss elements of story: character, setting, and plot and fill in the sheet.

- Writer's Corner: Write your Worm Story or another of your choosing. Be sure your story has a character, setting, and problem/plot.

Bark Walk

Tree Bark Rubbings

As you walk, create rubbings of four different varieties of tree by holding your paper against the trunk and shading lightly with a crayon or pencil.

Camouflage
or Mimicry

Animals use *camouflage* to blend in with their environment.
An animal using *mimicry* looks like (mimics) something else.

Camouflage

Mimicry

A white rabbit blends into the snow.

The walking stick looks like a stick.

My favorite animal that hides is:

It protects itself from predators by:

Adopt-a-Tree
plant a tree

My Tree

Word Bank

Crown	Roots	Trunk
Bole	Branch	Foliage

_____ *Dormant* means the tree is alive but slowed down as if sleeping. Most trees are dormant in winter months.

Hint: Ovals—crown (leafy top) and bole (trunk & base)

Soil! It's Alive

Collect a soil sample and draw it below.

Soil Experiment

1. Place a few Tablespoons of soil in a clear container.
2. Fill with water and stir.
3. Allow the soil to settle completely (give it time!).
4. Draw your observation.

With a magnifying glass, I see:

Worm Story

The Ws of Worms

Every story needs three elements. A Who (character), a Where (setting), and a Why (problem, goal, or plot). Imagine you're a worm and fill in the blanks below.

Who

Where

Why

Writer's Corner
Draw & Write

Story this!

Write a story and draw an illustration.

April

Welcome Spring!

This Month

Metaphor/Simile
Poetry
Weather & Graphs
Spring
Buds

Mama Earth's sunny smile cracks the last of April's ice along the river's edge.
—From A Year With Mama Earth

Me in Today's Weather:

Spring

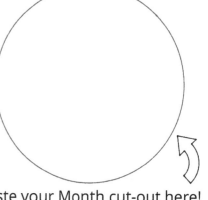

Paste your Month cut-out here!

April

Notes for Teachers

April topics:

Metaphor/Simile
Poetry
Weather & Graphs
Spring
Buds

*Mama Earth's sunny smile
cracks the last of April's ice
along the river's edge.*
—From A Year With Mama Earth

April showers bring May flowers, although April often begins with a blizzard where I live! The year I'm creating this resource is unique—many, many children are off school and public buildings and events are closed. How better to enjoy the first days of spring than by venturing outdoors?

Find suggestions for each activity page below.

- April: Add today's weather to your self portrait. How is the weather impacting what you wear today?

- Hey, Bud: Where appropriate, find a tree in bud and carefully examine using your magnifying glass. Be sure to use only what you need—buds will become the tree's leaves, which it needs to grow throughout the summer.

- Sense Spring: Can you smell spring in the air? Do you see signs? Collect or draw items from a nature walk (though please use your imagination for "taste").

- Weather: Practice observation, recording data, and graph-making by recording weather every day. You needn't record for a whole month. Choose a week or two and use your data to fill in the chart.

- Warm as: Learn about simile and metaphor with this activity. Make up your own similes and metaphors for extra fun!

- Writer's Corner: A Haiku is a traditional Japanese poem with three-lines and with seventeen syllables, written in a 5/7/5 syllable count.

- Writer's Bonus: Because April is National Poetry Month, use this bonus page to create an acrostic using your name!

Hey, Bud

What's happening?

Buds hold the building blocks for leaves. If you carefully open a bud, you may see tiny, baby leaves! Draw your bud and study it with a magnifying glass.

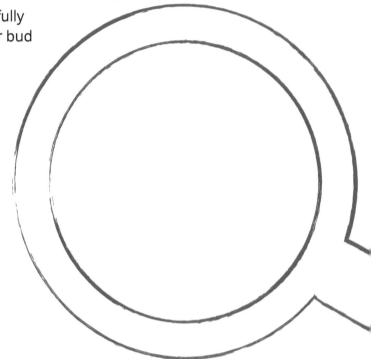

What do you think a full-grown leaf will look like? Draw your prediction (your hypothesis) and compare it in a few weeks to the grown leaf (observation).

Date: _____

Date: _____

Sense Spring!
Finally here!

Draw or paste a Sign of Spring you observed from each of your senses, plus a favorite.

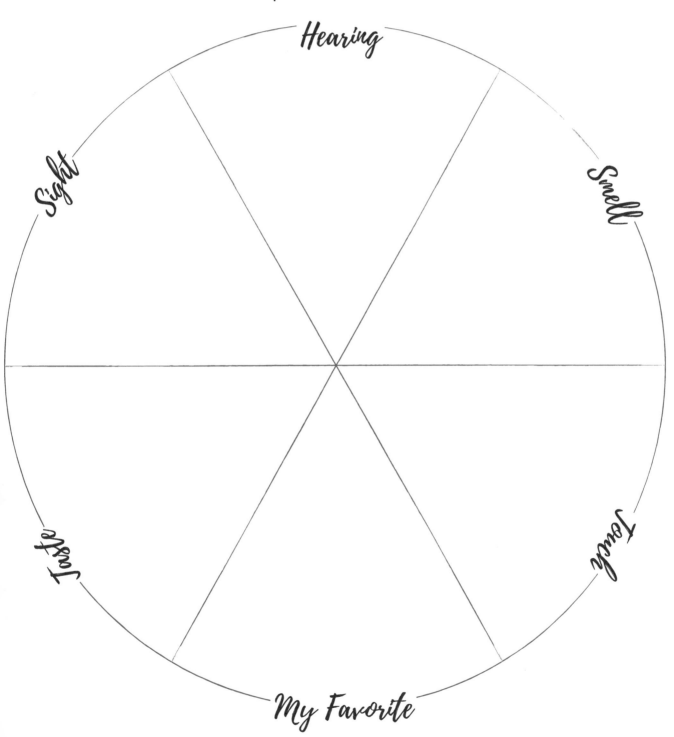

Hearing

Sight

Smell

Taste

Touch

My Favorite

Weather
Graphing

Record your observation each day for a week or for the whole month.

Sun	Mon	Tue	Wed	Thur	Fri	Sat

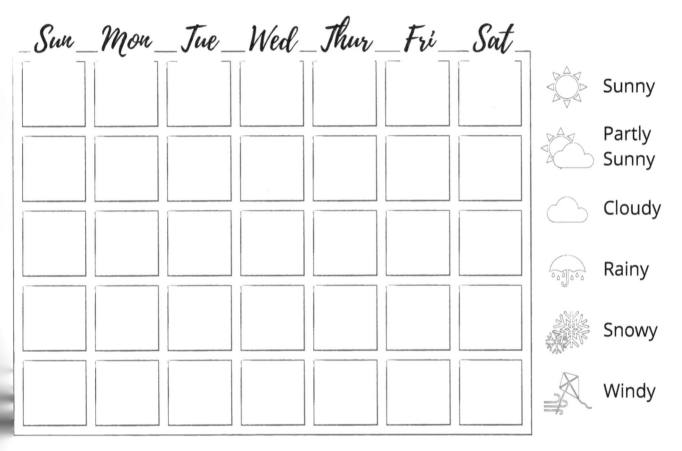

☀ Sunny

⛅ Partly Sunny

☁ Cloudy

☂ Rainy

❄ Snowy

🪁 Windy

Shade one block for each day of observed weather. What weather did you have the most?

Warm as. . .
Simile and metaphor

A simile is a comparison using the words like or as. A metaphor is a comparison without those words. Poetry often uses simile and metaphor. Create your own similes and metaphors below.

Cold as. . .

Warm like. . .

Rain is. . .

Writer's Corner

Draw & Write

A haiku is a short poem with three lines, 17 syllables in a 5-7-5 pattern. Most haiku are about nature. Visit rebeccagrabill.com/nature-journal to learn more about writing haiku.

My Haiku:

Writer's Bonus
Write more, write now

April is national poetry month. Create your own Name Acrostic! An acrostic is a poem using the letters of a word (you name or word of your choice) to begin each line. The lines may be single words or longer.

—— Illustrate your Acrostic By Drawing it with Fun Lettering Below ——

May

Spring Flowers!

This Month

Flowers & Seeds
Gardens
Life Cycle of a Flower
Decomposition
Recycling

*May perfumes Mama Earth
with violet
and honeysuckle.*
—From A Year With Mama Earth

Me as a Flower:

Flowers

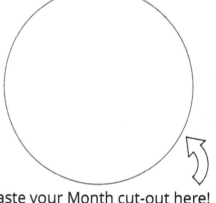

Paste your Month cut-out here!

May

Notes for Teachers

May topics:

Flowers & Seeds
Gardens
Life Cycle of a Flower
Decomposition
Recycling

*May perfumes Mama Earth
with violet
and honeysuckle.*
—From A Year With Mama Earth

May we go outdoors yet? Of course! Flowers, cute, baby plants, a garden full of promise. May is one of my favorite months. I hope you'll enjoying being outside as much as I will. Finally, no more snow where I live (usually)!

Find suggestions for each activity page below.

- May: April showers bring May ... flowers! Dress yourself as a flower this month. Which flower are you?

- Flowers: Label the parts of a flower, and use a field guide (or the internet) to identify your plant.

- Inside a Seed: You can do this page with any seed, but a larger seed (bean) is easiest. Try soaking several seeds and doing this and the Germination page together.

- Germination: Soak some fast-sprouting seeds (radish, dried beans) to watch the magic of germination happen! Continue your experiment if you'd like, but transfer the seedlings to soil so your plants can eat.

- Life Cycle: Plants and animals have a life cycle—birth, growth, reproduction. Discover a plant's life cycle from seed, through seedling, plant, flower and back to seed. Where's pollination? Stay tuned! We'll cover pollination in June.

- What Lasts? We all know about recycling, but how long does it take things we throw away to biodegrade? Does knowing the facts make you more or less interested in recycling?

- Decomposition: The process of a dead organism being broken down into its useful building blocks is fascinating and valuable for scientists who study soil.

- Writer's Corner: Like a garden, writing takes planning. Plan your imaginary garden by writing about it here!

Flowers

And their parts

Can you find a flower? Sketch it below and label the parts.

My flower:

Word bank:

flower

the way most plants reproduce through pollination

petals

the colorful part of a flower and sometimes smells sweet

stem

the strong part of a plant, it brings food from leaves and soil to make seeds

leaf

brings in water and turns sunlight and air into energy for a plant

roots

bring a plant water and minerals from the soil

Inside a Seed
A Tiny Power plant

My plant:

My seed:

What does your seed look like on the inside? Draw it in the magnifying glass.

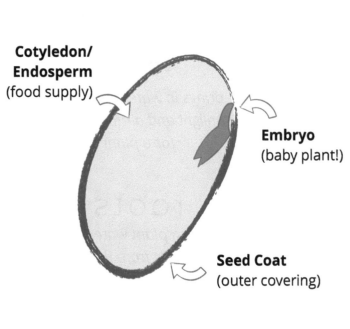

Cotyledon/ Endosperm
(food supply)

Embryo
(baby plant!)

Seed Coat
(outer covering)

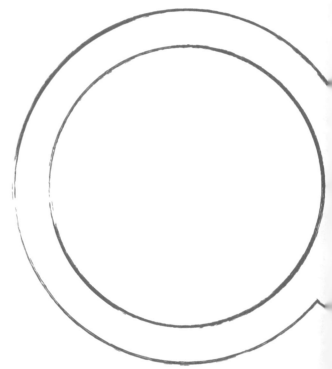

Germination

How seeds grow

Place a bean or radish seed in water and observe for several days. What do you see?

Day 1

Day 2

Day 3

Describe your observations below:

Can you identify these parts of the seed?
- **seed coat/embryo**
- **cotyledon**
- **root**
- **leaves**

Life Cycle
Story of a plant

Place a bean or radish seed in water and observe for several days. What do you see?

Many plants grow fruit after the flower is pollinated. The seeds are inside the fruit or vegetable.

seed

seedling

Can you find each part of the life cycle? Draw or collect.

flower

plant

What lasts?

The long life of trash

You probably already know that some things we throw away break down faster than others. Do you know how long these items take to biodegrade? Quiz yourself to find out!

A

milk carton ...

1. 1 week
2. 5 years
3. 500 years

B

plastic bottle ...

1. 6 weeks
2. 12 months
3. 450 years

C

paper towel ...

1. 2 weeks
2. 3 months
3. 100 years

D

apple core ...

1. 1 week
2. 2 months
3. 25 years

E

plastic bag ...

1. 10 weeks
2. 10 months
3. 10 years

F

glass ...

1. 2 weeks
2. 3 months
3. 1 million years

Going on a trash walk!

Walk through your neighborhood, a park, or your own house and collect trash. What gets recycled where, and what's thrown away? Use tally marks or write down an example of each.

Glass

Plastic

Paper

Metal

Compost

Trash

Answers: A2; B3; C1; D2; E3; F3

73

Decomposition
How life eats

Nature is always hungry. Microbes (bacteria), fungi (mushrooms, mold), and worms are **decomposers**. Decomposers are organisms that consume (eat) other dead organisms.

bacteria

worms

fungi

mold

Find something that is decomposing and sketch it below:

Writer's Corner

Draw & Write

What would you grow in your garden?

List your garden favorites:

June

From Spring to Summer

Bees
Wetlands
Food Webs
Parts of Speech

*In June, dizzy bees roll
in open blooms until their bodies
turn yellow with summer's sugar.*
—From *A Year With Mama Earth*

I'm ready to swim:

Summer

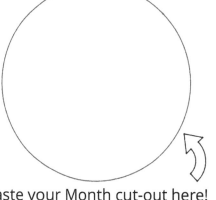

Paste your Month cut-out here!

June

Notes for Teachers

June topics:

Bees
Wetlands
Food Webs
Parts of Speech

In June, dizzy bees roll in open blooms until their bodies turn yellow with summer's sugar.
—From A Year With Mama Earth

June where I live brings dancing bees, fragrant roses, and thunder showers. It's sometimes finally warm enough to break out the sprinkler or wade in the creek. Wetlands come alive with eager life in June, which makes June a perfect month to visit a stream, marsh or other wetland. I hope you can get outside and enjoy those first breaths of summer!

Find suggestions for each activity page below.

- June: We usually have at least a day or two warm enough for water play. Draw yourself ready for the beach or a day in the sprinkler.

- Bees: Bees are fascinating. Spend some time following and watching them—from a distance! Did you know they communicate with one another through dance?

- Water Walk: Visit a wetland and play a game of I Spy. What do you see high, low, and at eye level?

- Wetland Webs: Food chains and webs are so much fun. Study the graphics and create your own food chain or web!

- Summer: Go on a summer scavenger hunt, collecting or drawing something for each box.

- Wordy World: Go on a nature walk and practice your parts of speech. What nouns, verbs, and adjectives can you find?

- Writer's Corner: Sometimes unexpected combinations create strange or funny or beautiful things. Take what you've learned about parts of speech and create your own mash-up. Use your words for a story, a character a drawing, or anything you'd like.

Bees

We're going on a bee hunt!

Draw bees where you find them in nature:

Bee tips

Be calm:
If a bee is making you nervous, hold still. The bee will likely fly away.

Be respectful:
Avoid stepping on flowers, openings to hives, or bees!

Be yourself:
Avoid perfume, scented lip gloss, and other things that might make you seem like bee food.

Water walk
I spy. . .

Visit a wetland, stream, pond, lake or other body of water and observe. What can you find?

Wetland webs
We are what we eat

A Food Chain shows the path one creature requires to reach food. A food web shows how different food chains relate to one another.

Food Chain   ### Food Web

My Food Chain or Web

Summer Scavenger Hunt!

flying insect

leafy tree

flower

songbird

eight-legged

small animal

seed or fruit

cloud

night creature

Wordy world
parts of speech

On a nature walk, notice all the parts of speech you experience or observe! Draw and write your words in the spaces provided below.

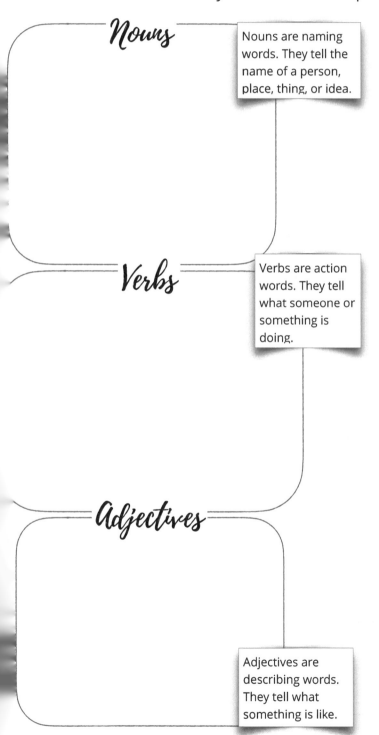

Nouns

Nouns are naming words. They tell the name of a person, place, thing, or idea.

Verbs

Verbs are action words. They tell what someone or something is doing.

Adjectives

Adjectives are describing words. They tell what something is like.

Writer's Corner

Draw & Write

Draw your Mash-Up!

Write three nouns, verbs, and adjectives, then circle one of each.
Write a sentence using all three circled words.

nouns	verbs	adjectives
1.	1.	1.
2.	2.	2.
3.	3.	3.

July

Our Outdoor World

This Month

**Fireflies & Insects
Night Creatures
Observation
Thermal Energy**

*July brings dancing rain,
and fireflies, and crickets
that sing till morning.*
—From A Year With Mama Earth

I'm dressed for summer:

Camping

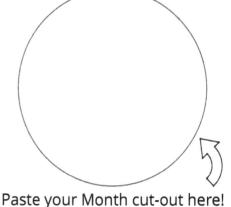

Paste your Month cut-out here!

July
Notes for Teachers

July topics:

Fireflies & Insects
Night Creatures
Observation
Thermal Energy

*July brings dancing rain,
and fireflies, and crickets
that sing till morning.*
—From A Year With Mama Earth

July brings fireflies and bonfires! I love s'mores and anything else I can cook over an open fire. I also love watching the mysterious dance of fireflies and the silhouettes of bats against the darkening night sky. Part of the fun of summer is enjoying long days and warm nights. I hope you can get outside, explore, observe, and enjoy nature this month!

Find suggestions for each activity page below.

- July: How do you dress for summer? Draw yourself here.

- Night Creatures: Study nocturnal, diurnal, and crepuscular animals by sorting them. Unsure of the definitions? Look at rebeccagrabill.com.

- Firefly Dance: Who doesn't love watching fireflies? The only thing more fun than watching is dancing with them! Use a flashlight or glow stick and show off your nighttime moves.

- Inspect it: Inspect an insect and draw and label its parts. Visit my website for great bug-observation tools.

- Hot Stuff: A great introduction to thermal energy. Discuss how light converts to heat and how dark colors absorb light while light colors reflect it. Which square melts your melty substance quickest?

- Day vs. Night: Stay out late some night this July. How is the world different from the daytime world? Be sure to use all your senses!

- Writer's Corner: What would you do all night long if you didn't have to sleep?

Firefly dance

into the night

Draw yourself as a firefly:

Did you know that fireflies glow to attract mates and to warn predators not to eat them? They're not tasty to bats or frogs.

Create your own firefly dance by going outside in the late evening with a flashlight and a scarf or play silk. Slowly float, turning your flashlight on and off. Try inventing patterns to communicate, like three flashes for *I Love You* or four for *Play Tag*.

Night Creatures

When are they awake?

Draw a line from the creature to its proper part of the Venn Diagram. Do you remember what *crepuscular* means? (Most active at dawn or dusk.)

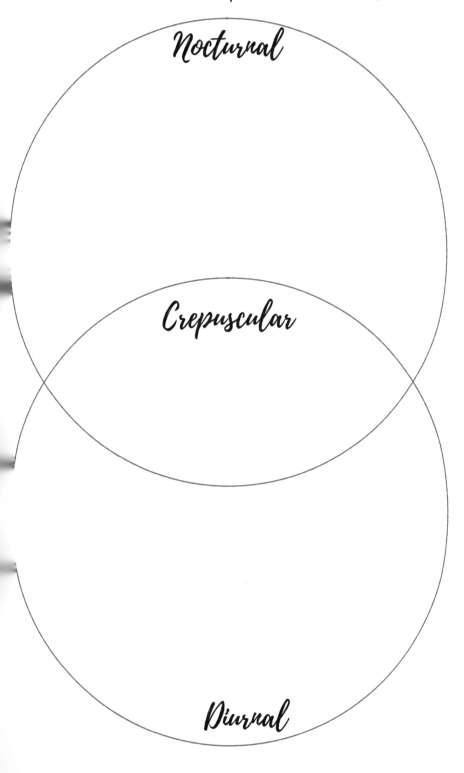

- moth
- bat
- mosquito
- robin
- owl
- firefly
- coyote
- deer
- raccoon
- rabbit
- butterfly
- squirrel
- human

Inspect it

Observing insects

Carefully observe an insect and record your observations. Does your insect have .

head	thorax	compound eyes	wings

legs	stinger	abdomen	antenna

A compound eye is made up of many tiny visual units.

What does your insect look like up close?

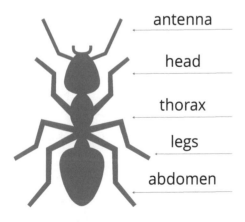

antenna

head

thorax

legs

abdomen

Hot Stuff
Melting away...

Place on piece of chocolate (or other melty item: cheese, crayon, ice, etc.) on each square.
Record your observations. Which melts faster? Why?

observations

1 minute

5 minutes

30

1 hour

3 hours

Day vs. Night

explore with senses

Spent time outdoors during the day, and again during the night (consider a camping trip!). Using your senses, what is different? What is the same?

Day

Night

touch *taste* sight
sound *taste* smell

Writer's Corner

Draw & Write

What would you do at night if you didn't need to sleep?

If I were nocturnal, I would ...

August

Beating Summer's Heat

Me keeping cool:

This Month

Sun & Shadows
Seasons
Rocks
Water Cycle

By August, her children have soaked the sun straight into their bones.
—From A Year With Mama Earth

Sunshine

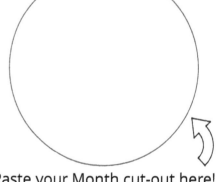

Paste your Month cut-out here!

August

Notes for Teachers

August topics:

Sun & Shadows
Seasons
Rocks
Water Cycle

By August, her children have soaked the sun straight into their bones.

—From A Year With Mama Earth

August brings dry grass, sizzling heat, and the first tastes of autumn's coming bounty. Learn about sun, seasons, shadows, and the water cycle this month with hands-on experiments and art lessons.

Find suggestions for each activity page below.

- August: How do you keep cool in the summer? Add it to your self portrait.

- Sundial: This easy activity could lead to discussions about to movement of the earth around the sun, seasonal weather changes, and more. Find activities and videos at rebeccagrabill.com.

- Shadow Art: Place your paper in an area of detailed shadow and practice tracing and shading. Are you surprised by your shadow art?

- Shadow Walk: You can collect shadows just as you would rocks or leaves! Look for texture in shadows and draw a different shadow in each box. You may be surprised by the variety of shadows you collect.

- Rock Out: Most of us have at least one collection. Try collecting rocks of different textures and colors. Can you identify the rock type? Talk about classification—how scientists organize all their vast knowledge.

- Water Cycle: Find many fun water cycle activities online and draw your own water cycle using the words provided. Evaporation is the process of liquid water becoming a gas, condensation involves gas collecting into water droplets as in a cloud, and precipitation is rain or snow.

- Writer's Corner: Summer is a time for making memories. What's your best summer memory? Capture it here to look back on years to come.

Sundial

Telling Time

1. Gather supplies—this page, clay, pencil.
2. Place a circle of clay in the center and stand the pencil up in it.
3. Set in a spot with consistent sun (you don't want to move it).

4. Trace the pencil's shadow and note the time.
5. Continue tracing the shadow once an hour for as long as you'd like.

Shadow Art
Tracing Beauty

Place this page in a shadow (under a leafy branch, by a fence, etc.) and trace the patterns. Color in the shadowy areas or paint as desired.

Shadow Walk
Seeing Space

Find shadows on a nature walk and sketch them in the panels below. Pay attention to both positive space (the shadow itself) and negative space (the light between shadows).

Rock Out

Collect and Sort

On a nature walk (or several), collect as many different types of rocks as you can. Uses the spaces below to sort or sketch your rocks by various attributes (color, size, texture).

Rocks come in all different shapes and sizes, but they can be classified into a few categories. How would you classify your rocks?

 formed by cooling magma; can be glassy or light and airy

igneous

 particles like sand and shells collect in layers and harden; can be crumbly

sedimentary

 pressure and slow-growing minerals give a ribbon-like look with shiny crystals

metamorphic

Water cycle
rain to cloud

Draw and label the water cycle using the word bank below.

Word Bank

evaporation   condensation   precipitation

Writer's Corner

Draw & Write

Draw your favorite summer memory below.

My favorite summer memory is ...

September

Welcome Autumn!

Seasons
Observation
Describing Words
Five Senses

*Mama Earth sighs and
September frost
crackles over bowing
stalks of corn...*
—From *A Year With Mama Earth*

Me in the Fall!

Autumn

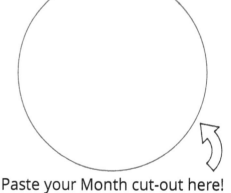

Paste your Month cut-out here!

September

Notes for Teachers

September's topics:

Seasons
Observation
Describing Words
Five Senses

Mama Earth sighs and September frost crackles over bowing stalks of corn...

—From *A Year With Mama Earth*

September is such a wonderful month. The air grows cooler, and the days are full of fall scents and back-to-school excitement.

Below find suggestions for each activity page.

- September: Draw yourself as you are today, in September. Trace the word, *Autumn*, and note the spelling. Did you know that *Fall* and *Autumn* are synonyms—they mean the same thing?

- Seasons: Collect tiny objects while enjoying nature. Dandelion fluff, leaves, grass, bits of clover. Glue them to the season sheet on the appropriate tree, or decorate with crayons, stickers, paints, etc.

- My Senses: On a nature walk, choose one plant or other natural object. Observe and fill in the blanks. Please do NOT taste anything unless you know it is edible, and identify potentially poisonous plants/insects before touching anything. *Optional*: use a field guide to identify your plant!

- I Spy: Look around and identify natural things you see. Clouds, trees, birds up high, and soil and bugs down low, etc.

- Up Close: Choose a natural object such as a plant, flower, rock, shell, piece of tree bark, leaf, etc. If possible, paste it in the space provided. If not, sketch or include a picture. Using a magnifying glass, study your object and sketch the tiny details.

- Writer's Corner: Choose a treasure on your nature walk. Use vivid descriptive words (adjectives) to write about your treasure.

Seasons

Through the Year

Decorate the trees to match the seasons!

Winter, Spring, Summer, Fall, I like _____ best of all!

Summer

Autumn

Winter

Spring

My Senses

Observation

My Plant

Looks like ...

mells like ...   Sounds like ...   Feels like ...

astes like ... ?

o NOT taste any plants or berries unless an adult tells you it's safe!! Instead, use our *imagination*. What do you imagine your plant might taste like?

I Spy

With My Little Eye...

What do you see up high?

Up High

What do you see at eye-level?

At My Eye

Down Low

What do you see down low?

132

Up Close
Magnifying

My object looks like this:

With a magnifying glass, I see:

Writer's Corner
Draw & Write

Draw and describe a treasure you discovered in nature!

My treasure is:

October

Happy Harvest Time!

This Month

Leaves
The Color Wheel
Personification
Spiders

Carved and lit from within, October's pumpkins grin.
—From A Year With Mama Earth

Dressed for Fall!

Harvest

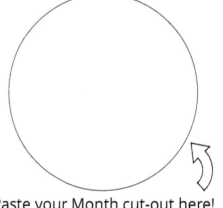

Paste your Month cut-out here!

October

Notes for Teachers

October in many areas is all about leaves and colors! And it's the perfect month to really explore nature. Temperatures are still pleasant, and wildlife abounds! In some areas, animals are busy preparing for winter or soaking up a shorter day's sun.

This month bring gallon-sized zipper bags.

Below find suggestions for each activity page.

- October: Do you dress differently for the weather in October? Or would you like to draw yourself dressed as favorite creature?

- Leaf Rubbings: Create a colorful keepsake by making leaf rubbing. You might enjoy making rubbings of other things like bark, rocks, wood, etc. Bring extra paper, because one will not be enough!

- Leaf identification: You'll likely also need a field guide or plant identification app. Discuss how close observation helps us recognize leaves, and try to collect one of each type!

- Color Wheel: As you walk look for or collect somethin in each color of the wheel. Talk about the variety of colors found in nature.

- Spiders: Spiders are everywhere! And their webs are nature's lace. Find and study these treasures, but always be careful not to disturb spiders or their habitats.

- Writer's Corner: What is *personification*? It's giving a non-human object/creature human qualities. That's what we're practicing in this month's Writer's Corner!

October's topics:

Leaves
The Color Wheel
Personification
Spiders

Carved and lit from within, October's pumpkins grin.
—From A Year With Mama Earth

Leaves

Make Leaf Rubbings

Place a leaf beneath your paper.
Rub over the paper with the side of a crayon or shade lightly with a pencil.

More Leaves

Identifying Leaves

Circle the leaf below that best matches yours:

Simple

Oak   Beech   Aspen   Maple   Ginko

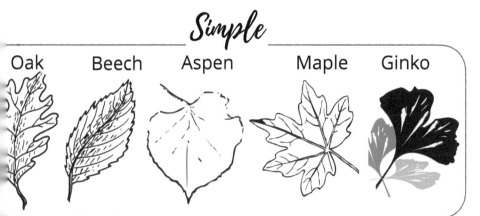

Simple leaves have one leaf per stem.

Compound

Ash   Palm

Compound leaves have multiple leaves per stem.

Lobed

Lobed leaves have deep bumps along the sides, like stubby fingers.

toothed

Toothed leaves have jagged edges, like the teeth on a saw (or a big cat!).

toothless

This leaf is toothless and lobed. The edges are smooth, but are split into large lobes like fingers.

My leaf looks like this:

Colorful
Autumn

Draw or paste something you found from each color of the color wheel.

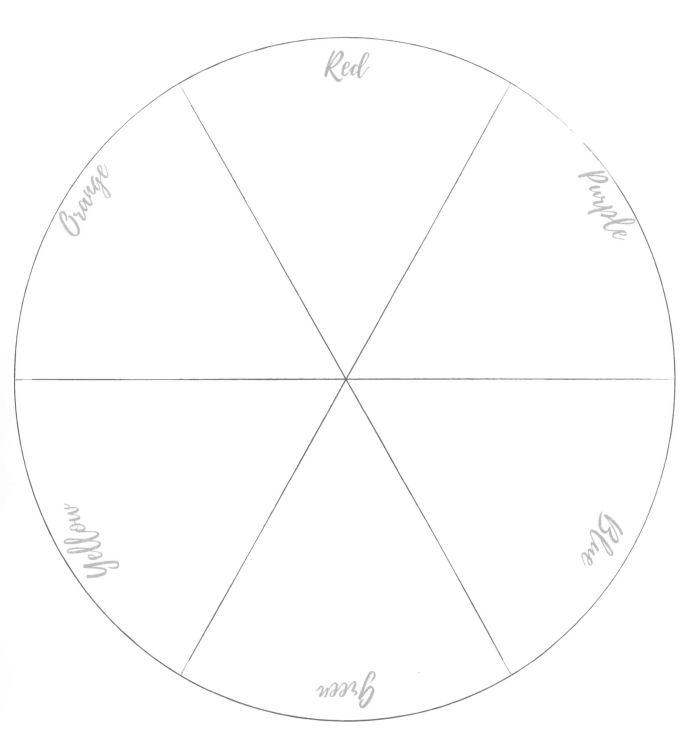

Spiders

And their amazing webs!

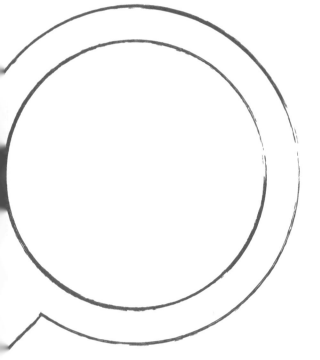

Draw your spider here!

Study your spider or web up close.

Can you draw a spider web?

Writer's Corner
Draw & Write

Draw and describe what your spider web would be like!

If I were a spider:

November

Give thanks with all your heart!

This Month

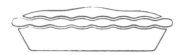

Gratitude
Clouds
Nature Mandalas
Winter Habitats

The busy squirrel packs the last few nuts into his summer stores.
—From A Year With Mama Earth

What will you wear?

Thankful

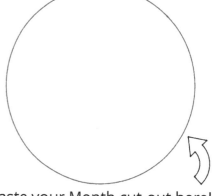

Paste your Month cut-out here!

November

Notes for Teachers

November topics:

Gratitude
Clouds
Nature Mandalas
Winter Habitats

The busy squirrel packs the last few nuts into his summer stores.

—From A Year With Mama Earth

Where I live, November winds blow the last of autumn's leaves across the lawn and children check the windows each morning, hoping to see the season's first snow. Nature walks involve bundling up, and almost always end with hot cocoa!

Below find suggestions for each activity page.

- November: Many families gather in November to celebrate togetherness and say Thank You for the gifts of love and life. Some dress up or travel. What will you wear as you celebrate fall?

- Gratitude Walk: Learn three Latin words: *Flora, Fauna,* and *Biota*. Collect or draw favorites in each category as you walk!

- Cloud Journal: For five days, note the clouds in the sky. The most common types of clouds are shown. Which do you see most?

- In the Sky: Use your imagination to pretend to ride a cloud! Would you float? Fly? Bounce? What does it feel like—texture; what does it smell like? Draw yourself in a cloud.

- Nature Mandala: Detailed instructions and video are available at rebeccagrabill.com/nature-journal. Collect objects: pine cones, leaves, rocks, feathers, etc. Arrange on the ground in a pleasing shape, practicing symmetry.

- Ready for Winter: Complete the worksheet to learn about hibernation, migration, and adaptation.

- Writer's Corner: Write a Thank-You letter to someone you care about!

Gratitude
Nature Walk

As you walk, reflect on gratitude. What are you most thankful for? Draw or paste items that remind you to say, *Thank You* for our beautiful Earth!

Flora

Fauna

Biota

Flora means plant life ~ *Fauna* means animal life ~ *Biota* means anything living

Cloudy sky
Journal

Record your observation each day. What type of cloud do you see the most?

Clear

Monday   Tuesday   Wednesday   Thursday   Friday

Cumulus

Monday   Tuesday   Wednesday   Thursday   Friday

Stratus

Monday   Tuesday   Wednesday   Thursday   Friday

Cirrus

Monday   Tuesday   Wednesday   Thursday   Friday

In the Sky

Imagination & art!

Draw yourself in a cloud. Are you walking or jumping, floating, flying, bouncing? What colors are in the cloud? What does the ground look like beneath you?

Mandala
Create a Fall Arrangement!

Collect treasures on your nature walk: Rocks, sticks, feathers, leaves and more. Arrange geometrically to create your own Fall Mandala! Draw your Mandala below.

Symmetry means "same" — when objects are symmetrical they are arranged identically on both sides, or are equally spaced around an axis.

Preparing
For Winter

Match each creature with its winter home and label from the word bank below.

Word Bank

Migrate   Hibernate   Adapt

Writer's Corner
Draw & Write

Draw someone you love and write a Thank You note!

Thank You for Loving Me!

December

Sharing with others.

This Month

Constellations
Evergreens
Pine Cones
Gift-giving & Lists

*In December,
Mama Earth dons her
winter coat.*
—From A Year With Mama Earth

Dress for winter!

Celebrate

Paste your Month cut-out here!

December

Notes for Teachers

December topics:

Constellations
Evergreens
Pine Cones
Gift-giving & Lists

*In December,
Mama Earth dons her
winter coat.*
—From A Year With Mama Earth

Ah, December. The month of sparkly lights, gift-giving, and overflowing to-do lists. Set some time aside to enjoy nature with this month's journal pages.

You'll be observing, making gifts, collecting treasures, and exploring your winter world!

Find suggestions for each activity page below.

- December: Trace the word *Celebrate* and get your monthly self-portrait dressed for winter! Talk about winter clothing and how we dress for the weather.

- Star Wash: Make a watercolor resist of the starry night. Discussion might include water soluble substances (not wax from crayons!), stars, and the movement of sun and planets.

- Constellations: Create your own constellation with natural objects! Talk about shapes in the sky and practice identifying constellations on a clear night.

- Inside a Pine Cone: Collect a seed pod or pinecone and take it apart. Closed pinecones will have seeds within, but open ones have already dropped their seeds. Look at rebeccagrabill.com/nature-journal for more crafts.

- All the Trees: Explore the differences and similarities between coniferous and deciduous trees and create a Venn Diagram using numbers, drawings, or collected items.

- Treasure Box: The ultimate in upcycling! Collect saved holiday cards and transform them into adorable tiny gift boxes.

- Writer's Corner: Lists are a wonderful starting point for creative writing. Use your lists to inspire more writing like poems or stories!

Star Wash

The Starry Sky

Did you know a group of stars that form a shape are called a constellation? Make your own constellation star wash! 1. Draw stars with CRAYON. Be sure to press hard. 3. Paint over your stars with watercolor paints or color over with marker.

Constellations
Make Your Own

Below is *Ursa Major.* That's Latin for Big Bear. You can make your own constellation by arranging stones, pine cones, or leaves on the ground. What shape will you make? Draw and name your constellation below!

Ursa Major

My Constellation:

Inside...
A Pine Cone

Collect pine cones (or other local seed pods) on your walk. Carefully peel away the outer layers. Draw your pine cone and what you find inside below.

All the Trees
Deciduous vs. Coniferous

Write the letter in the proper part of the Venn Diagram. Bonus: draw your answers!

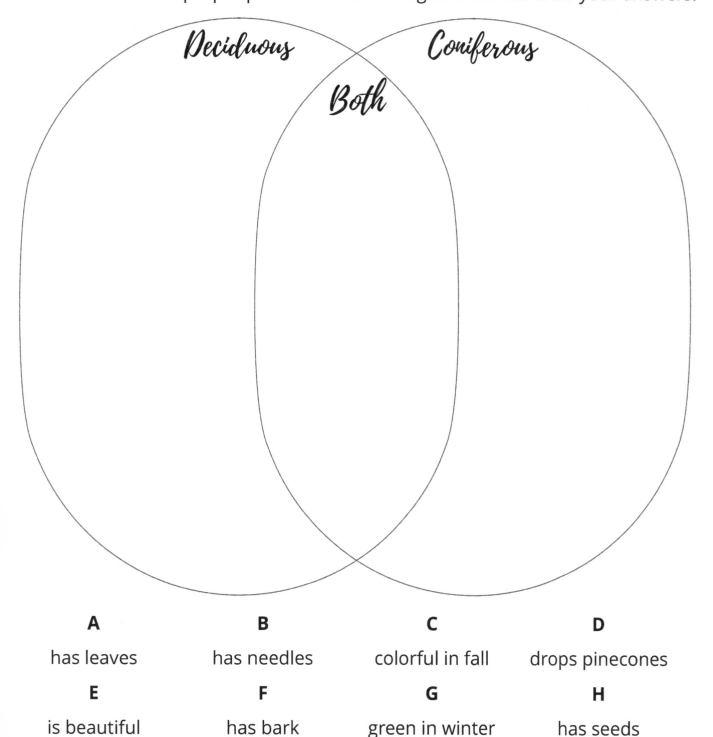

Deciduous   **Both**   **Coniferous**

A	**B**	**C**	**D**
has leaves	has needles	colorful in fall	drops pinecones
E	**F**	**G**	**H**
is beautiful	has bark	green in winter	has seeds

Treasure Box
For Holiday Gift-Giving

Make tiny boxes from greeting cards or heavy paper. Fill with delights and gift to all the your favorite people. Who will receive a special gift from you?

step 1 Cut a square from a greeting card. Tip: fold one corner in to the opposite side to form a square. (If you don't want creases in the lid, measure a square.)

step 2 Fold each of the corners in to meet in the center. (If you measured your square, find center by connecting the corners with lines on the back side.)

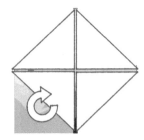

step 3 Fold the straight edges inward toward the center, unfolding and repeating on the other side.

 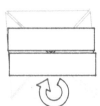 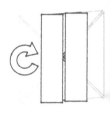

step 4 Unfold completely. Your paper should look something like this. Mark along the solid lines and snip ONLY to the second fold! Cut and discard the gray triangles.

 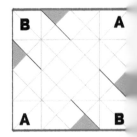

step 5 1. Refold corners A to the center. 2. Fold the snipped tabs inward to make the sides of your box. 3. Fold corners B OVER the tabs to make your box!

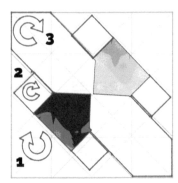

Repeat for the bottom, but make your square approximately 1/4-1/2 inch smaller.

top

Box Template
DIY Gift Boxes

1. Cut out or copy on heavy card stock.
2. Cut out.
3. Decorate non-printed side.
4. Fold per instructions.
5. Snip on solid lines; discard shaded triangles.
6. Re-fold.
7. Fill!

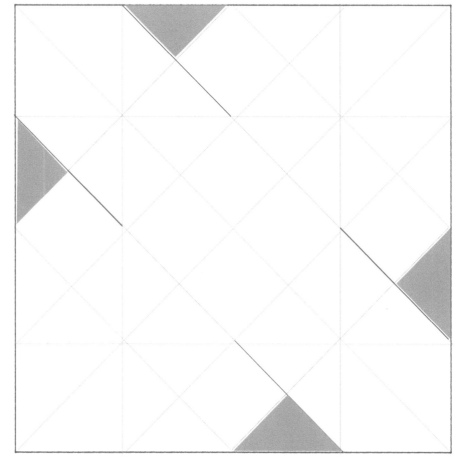

bottom

Writer's Corner
Draw & Write

Draw some of your favorite winter things!

How many winter things can you list? Circle your favorites.

All Seasons

Senses Scavenger Hunt!

Something Loud

Something Smelly

Something Rough

Something Pretty

Something Cold

Something Quiet

Something Smooth

Something Green

Something Wet

All Seasons

Senses Scavenger Hunt!

Something Dry

Something Fresh

Something Warm

Something Bumpy

Something Weird

Something Silent

Something Gritty

Something Red

Something Soft

Thank you for supporting
My Year Nature Journal

I love this! Where can I find more of your books?

I'm so glad you asked! I have all my books as well as printables and activities galore listed on my website, https://www.rebeccagrabill.com.

Three of my books are *Violet and the Woof* (HarperCollins), *A Year With Mama Earth* (Eerdmans), and *Halloween Good Night* (Atheneum).

What else do you offer?

I've created oodles of resources to help you use literature in the classroom!

✳ Printable Packs

✳ Coloring Pages

✳ Crafts and Games

✳ Educational Resources

✳ Lesson Plans

One last thing...

I would LOVE to hear from you. Please tag me on social media @rebeccawritesbooks or with #myyearnaturejournal or send me stories, artwork, letters at rebeccawritesbooks@gmail.com

Don't forget to order my books!!

Made in United States
Troutdale, OR
10/29/2024

24265436R00106